A Little

Coffee Cookbook

Janet Laurence

ILLUSTRATED BY CATHERINE McWILLIAMS

Chronicle Books

First published in 1992 by
The Appletree Press Ltd,
19–21 Alfred Street, Belfast BT2 8DL
Copyright © 1992 The Appletree Press, Ltd.
Printed in the E.U. All rights reserved.
No part of this publication may be reproduced or
transmitted in any form or by means, electronic or
mechanical, photocopying, recording or any
information and retrieval system, without
permission in writing from the publisher.

A Little Coffee Cookbook

First published in the United States in 1992 by
Chronicle Books, 275 Fifth Street,
San Francisco, CA 94103

ISBN: 0-8118-0256-6

9 8 7 6 5 4 3 2

A note on measures
Spoon measurements are level except where
otherwise indicated. Seasonings can be adjusted
according to taste. Recipes are for four
unless otherwise indicated.

Introduction

Coffee offers a rich and potent experience. Its powerful and haunting flavor and aroma are instantly recognizable yet, so many and so varied are the blends offered, few cups are the same. Its mystique confounds many but making a good cup of coffee is simplicity itself. Its powers of stimulation can be as addictive as its lively and subtle flavor; coffee is the thinking person's drink and one of the sophisticated cook's favorite flavorings. Coffee first grew wild in Ethiopia. Originally a kind of wine made from the fermented bean pulp, it was known by the poetic Arabic word for wine, "qahweh". Later the beans were roasted and pulverized and the powder whipped into hot water. Coffee offered stimulation without the taint of forbidden alcohol and pilgrims spread its use throughout the Islamic world.

The Venetians brought coffee to Europe in 1615, with instant success. Over the next hundred years, coffee houses opened in many major cities, providing meeting places for businessmen, politicians, journalists, artists, and intellectuals. Revolutions were said to have been fermented in cafes, commercial institutions grew out of them and they became fashionable centers for refreshment and gossip. In America, the Tea Tax and the Boston Tea Party linked coffee indelibly in the American mind with liberty and democracy.

Coffee has been claimed to be both beneficial and harmful. Caffeine in small doses can improve attention, concentration and co-ordination and, in excess, can produce over-acute sensations, irregular heartbeats and muscular trembling. Like most great things in life, coffee is best enjoyed in moderation.

The Cultivation of Coffee

The Arabs tried to maintain a monopoly on the production of coffee by refusing to allow plants or unsterilized berries to leave their shores, but seeds and small plants were soon smuggled out. In the seventeenth century, coffee began to be grown in India and the Far East Dutch colonies such as Java and Ceylon. Later it reached the West Indies and South America where Brazil, in particular, provided ideal conditions.

In the second half of the nineteenth century, *Hemileia vastatrix,* a devastating leaf disease, struck Asia and moved on to Africa, wiping out the coffee trees. Brazil took over as pre-eminent grower, a position it maintained after cultivation was re-established in Africa and Asia and still holds today, when coffee is grown wherever there is a suitable climate.

There are two species of coffee tree. *Coffee arabica* is the original and produces beans of a more complex, interesting flavor. *Coffee canephora,* also known as *robusta,* is easier to cultivate and can be grown in warmer and lower regions; it is used mainly in some instant coffees. Roughly speaking, the higher coffee is grown, the better its flavor.

Coffee trees resemble laurel bushes and bear beautiful, sweet smelling white flowers at the same time as the berries are ripening. Each berry usually contains two flat-sided seeds or beans. A single bean is round, known as a peaberry. Picked when red and about the size of a cherry, the berry pulp has to be softened so the beans can be separated before being cleaned, dried, graded, and then shipped.

Coffee's distinctive flavor and color are developed by roasting, a process which needs nice judgement and varies according to the desired taste. Different coffee varieties yield different degrees of

aroma, body, acidity, and color and expert tasters develop blends to suit different tastes and purposes.

Roasting Degrees:
Light or pale: mild coffee with a delicate flavor, good with milk and ideal for breakfast.
Medium: more character with a stronger flavor.
Full or dark: a strong, full-bodied flavor.
High, double or continental: very strong, accentuates coffee's bitter aspects and often loses some of the original flavor, should be drunk black.

Varieties:
Today over fifty countries produce more than 100 varieties of coffee. Specialty shops offer carefully selected blends of arabica beans, some of the best come from:
Brazil: Most prized is Santos, a sweet, clear, neutral flavor.
Columbia: The Andes foothills produces some of the finest coffees. Look for: Medellins, Excelso, Manizales, Armenias, Libanos, Bogotas and Bucaramangas.
Costa Rica: Excellent coffees, particularly those from the Central Plateau, with a rich body and fine, mild flavor.
Jamaica: High grown Blue Mountain is most expensive and highly prized coffee in the world.
Kenya: Excellent flavor and fine acidity, the peaberry's round shape allows for even roasting.
Mocha: The Yemeni seaport from which coffee was first exported gave its name to highly popular Ethiopian beans.
Mysore: Indian coffees with a distinctive, soft, acid flavor.
Decaffeinated: Recently popular, available varieties have increased and flavor has improved. The caffeine is removed either through steaming (the Swiss method) or a solvent.

Instant: Freshly brewed liquid is either evaporated or freeze dried, the latter is considered to give the better result.
Organic: A tiny proportion of the coffee available but a rapidly growing market.

Making Coffee

Coffee's flavor comes from volatile oils that start deteriorating immediately after roasting and grinding accelerates the process. So buy in small quantities and, if possible, grind just before using or keep opened packets tightly closed. Vacuum packs conserve flavor, so does keeping in the freezer. Maximum flavor comes from steeping coffee grounds for two minutes in water at a temperature just below boiling. As a general rule, use one tablespoon of grounds per scant $1/2$ cup of freshly drawn water. Dilute with hot water or milk for weaker coffee. Drink as soon as possible, flavor and aroma are both volatile. Keep equipment spotlessly clean, as coffee oil residue turns rancid.

Jug or cafetière. Simplest of all methods. Warm either, add medium ground coffee, pour on hot water. When using a jug give a good stir, leave two minutes then strain or spoon over a little cold water to settle grounds. With a cafetière, leave two minutes then slowly push down plunger, never force it.
Filter. Fit special filter paper into the cone, place on top of a jug, add finely ground coffee and a little hot water to moisten. Then slowly pour on rest of hot water. Electric machines are available but some over-extract coffee and give a bitter flavor. Single portion "cafe filters" should be placed over a warmed cup.

Drip. A three-part coffee jug. Place finely ground coffee in middle, pour hot water in the top and allow to filter through to the bottom part. A metal kind allows the water to be heated on the stove, then the pot is reversed for the filter process.

Cona. Two glass bowls are connected via a glass funnel and filter and held in a stand over a spirit lamp. The water is heated in the bottom bowl to boiling point, and then rises into the upper bowl, which holds finely ground coffee. Give it a good stir, remove the heat and allow the coffee to filter through to the bottom bowl. Remove top bowl before serving.

Percolator. Place medium ground coffee in the basket, fill percolator with fresh water and heat until steam forces the water repeatedly through the stem and over the coffee. Electric percolators time the process automatically. Purists maintain this method over-extracts the coffee, producing a bitter result.

Espresso. A mixture of steam and water at higher temperature then normal is forced through very finely ground coffee, producing a stronger brew than the above methods and a layer of froth. To make cappuccino, add a mixture of hot milk and steam on top of plain espresso; grated chocolate or cinnamon is almost always added as a finishing touch.

Turkish and Arabian. A strong, slightly bitter coffee that is usually served sweetened. Boil 2 teaspoons of sugar (or to taste) with one small coffee cup of water in either a traditional *ibrik*, a small brass pot with a narrow top and long handle, or a small saucepan. Add 2 teaspoons very finely ground coffee, stirring well. Heat again until the coffee froths up, remove pot from heat and allow to settle then repeat twice more. Allow to settle again then serve. A cardamom pod or a clove or two or a pinch of freshly grated nutmeg can be added to the water before boiling.

Coffee Drinks

Iced Coffee. There are more ways of drinking coffee than straight and hot. Iced coffee can be made by cooling a freshly made brew in the refrigerator then serving to taste with sugar, or honey, and cream. But on really hot days it is most refreshing made extra strong and poured over ice cubes.

---

freshly made, double strength coffee
equal quantity ice cubes
sugar or honey to taste
cream

Make the coffee, allow to cool, then pour over ice cubes, sweeten to taste with sugar or honey then add cream and stir.

Spiced Coffee. Most spirits and liqueurs accompany coffee beautifully and a number will lace it equally well. Add sugar, even if you normally take coffee without, the spirit makes it bitter otherwise. This is the ultimate alcoholic coffee.

$1/2$ cup brandy
3 tbsp sugar
10 whole cloves, $1/2$ in piece cinnamon stick
thinly pared peel of 1 lemon and 1 orange
one third of a vanilla bean
4 cups black coffee, freshly made
(serves 6–8 people)

Place all the ingredients except the coffee, which should be kept hot, in a stainless steel or enamel saucepan and heat gently until sugar dissolved and brandy warm enough to light. Ignite then pour coffee over, warm through if necessary, and strain into coffee cups.

Irish Coffee. If Spiced Coffee is the ultimate, Irish is the favorite after-dinner alcoholic coffee, simple but utterly delicious. I remember a bar in San Francisco in the sixties that lined up the glassed along the counter to make twenty or so Irish Coffees at a time. Don't use too delicate a glass and choose a medium-dark roast for your coffee, otherwise the flavor of the whisky will prove too powerful.

---

1 hefty wine goblet, warmed
2 tbsp Irish whisky
1 tsp, or more, of brown sugar
freshly-brewed strong, medium-dark roast coffee
2 tbsp heavy cream
(makes 1)

Place the whisky in the bottom of the glass, add the sugar and place a spoon in the glass. Pour the coffee over the spoon and stir to dissolve the sugar. Hold the spoon just above the level of the coffee, rounded side up, and carefully pour over the cream so it floats on the surface of the coffee. Don't stir, the idea is to drink the whisky-fortified coffee through the smooth richness of the cream. Heaven.

Caffe Sambuca. The Italians have a special trick with their liqueur Sambuca, made from liquorice and elderflower.

---

1 liqueur glass Sambuca
3 or 5 dark roasted coffee beans
1 match
(makes 1)

Float the coffee beans on top of the liqueur. Light with a match and allow to burn for a few seconds then blow out (be gentle) and sip the liqueur which is now faintly flavored with freshly-roasted coffee. The *cognoscenti* crunch the beans as they sip.

Marinated Mushrooms

Full of a robust and tantalizing flavor, these mushrooms make a good starter or side salad.

8oz button mushrooms, trimmed
3 tbsp fresh lemon juice
1 cup medium-strength black coffee
3 tbsp groundnut, peanut or arachide oil
small bunch parsley stalks, a sprig thyme
and 1 celery stalk, all tied together
1 tsp coriander seeds
2 crushed cloves garlic
1/2 tsp salt, little freshly-ground black pepper
freshly chopped parsley

Add mushrooms and lemon juice to a saucepan of boiling water and blanch for five minutes. Drain and refresh in cold water. Bring remaining ingredients, apart from the chopped parsley, to boil and simmer gently for five minutes. Add the drained mushrooms, bring back to boil then remove from heat, place in suitable container and leave to marinate at least six hours or, better, overnight. Sprinkle with chopped parsley before serving with crusty bread or wholemeal toast.

Coffee and Chestnut Pâté

A pâté with an interesting texture and a subtle, autumnal flavor.

---

1 small onion, finely chopped
1 clove garlic, crushed
1 tbsp groundnut, peanut or arachide oil
2 celery stalks, finely chopped
12oz cooked chestnuts, roughly chopped
15oz can unsweetened chestnut purée
7 tbsp strong black coffee
2 eggs, lightly beaten
little salt, freshly-ground black pepper
bay leaf
(serves 8)

Gently fry the onion and garlic in the oil until soft. Mix with the celery and chopped chestnuts.

Mix together the chestnut purée, coffee, eggs and seasoning. Stir in the chopped chestnut mixture.

Grease a 2 lb loaf pan or round dish of similar volume and place the bay leaf in the bottom. Add the pâté mixture, pressing down firmly. Cover with two layers of aluminum foil, fastening it round the edges of the pan. Place pâté in a roasting pan and add sufficient cold water to come halfway up the loaf pan. Bake in a preheated oven at 325°F for 1 1/2–2 hours. Remove mold from heat and leave to cool on a rack for several hours before turning out.

Spicy Chicken

The coffee combines with the spices and liver to make a rich, fragrant sauce that defies analysis. Freshly ground spices will improve the flavor.

---

1 chicken, 3½ lbs, jointed, reserve liver
1 tsp powdered cinnamon
1 tsp ground cumin
pinch ground mace
10 fl oz black coffee, medium strong
salt
2 tbsp cream, preferably double
2oz toasted almonds

Mix together the spices and rub over the surface of the chicken pieces. Place in a plastic bag, pour over the strained coffee and arrange the bag in a bowl so that the chicken is immersed in the coffee. Leave in a cool place overnight.

Place chicken leg pieces in a shallow roasting dish, pour over the marinade, add salt and cook, uncovered, in a preheated oven at 350°F for 15 minutes, then baste and add breast pieces and the liver and continue cooking for another 30 minutes, or until chicken is cooked, basting with the coffee juices.

Remove the cooked chicken and keep warm. Skim juices of all fat, add the cooked liver and blend in a food processor or push through a sieve. Pour into a clean pan, adjust seasoning then reheat to just below boiling point. Stir in the cream, remove from heat and pour over the chicken. Garnish with the toasted almonds and serve.

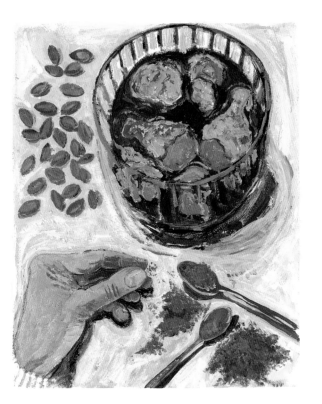

Lamb Roasted With Coffee

This is a traditional Swedish recipe. The coffee cuts the fatty quality of the lamb and produces delicious gravy but is quite unrecognizable in the finished dish.

$4^1/_2$ lb leg of lamb
little butter or oil
salt and freshly-ground black pepper
generous cup coffee, medium strength, mixed with 2 tbsp light cream
and 1 tsp sugar
Sauce:
2 tbsp flour
additional light cream or milk
1 tsp redcurrant jelly
(serves 6)

Rub meat with butter or oil, season well. Place in roasting pan and roast in preheated oven at 400°F for 10 minutes. Reduce heat to 350°F and continue roasting for one hour, basting every 20 minutes. Then add the white, sweetened coffee to the pan and continue roasting for another hour, or until joint cooked to your liking, basting as before. When done, remove meat and keep warm.

Strain the pan juices then skim fat off the top and return 2 tablespoons to the roasting pan with the 2 tablespoons of flour. Cook over a moderate heat for a few minutes, stirring all the time, then make a smooth sauce with the degreased juices and redcurrant jelly, made up to 2 cups with additional light cream or milk, scraping the bottom of the roasting pan well to incorporate any crusty bits with all their flavor. Adjust seasoning, simmer 5–10 minutes then serve with the meat.

Coffee Cheesecake

This is a cooked cheesecake, rich and really scrumptious, with the coffee and cheese blending perfectly.

Base:	²/₃ cup heavy cream
2 cups Graham crackers, crushed	¹/₂ tsp vanilla essence
I stick butter, melted	I¹/₂ tbsp coffee essence
pinch ground cinnamon	**Topping:**
Filling:	generous ¹/₂ cup (I carton)
2¹/₂ cups curd or cream cheese	soured cream
I cup superfine sugar	I tbsp superfine sugar
3 eggs, well beaten	

(serves 8)

To make the base, mix together the crushed crackers, melted butter and ground cinnamon and use to line the bottom of a greased 8 in diameter pan with a removable base and, if possible, a spring-clip side.

To make the filling, cream together cheese and sugar, then gradually beat in the eggs. Stir in the cream, the vanilla and the coffee essence. Pour onto the base and bake in a preheated oven at 325°F for 30 minutes, until the filling is set. Turn off the oven and leave to cool.

To finish, mix together the sour cream and sugar and spread over the top of the cheesecake. Heat oven to 425°F then bake the cheesecake for about 5 minutes, until the topping has formed a glaze. Remove and chill for several hours, preferably overnight. Carefully release from pan before serving.

Petits Pôts de Crème au Mocha

The Venetians invented the exquisite combination of coffee and chocolate, calling it *mocha*. A full-bodied but mild coffee is best for this recipe.

---

2 cups full-cream milk
2 tbsp coffee, coarsely ground
2oz bitter chocolate, broken into pieces
3 tbsp superfine sugar
5 large egg yolks

Heat the milk and coffee to just below boiling point, remove from heat, cover and allow to infuse for several minutes. Strain through a fine sieve. Add the sugar and the pieces of chocolate and stir until the chocolate is thoroughly melted. Add the egg yolks to the milk mixture, stirring in at the same time. Pour the egg mixture into ramekin dishes or little custard pots, covering with lids if available (the pots will probably hold more custard than the ramekins). Place in a roasting pan and add cold water to just above half way up the pots. Place in a preheated oven at 325°F for 40–50 minutes until the custards are set. A little cream poured over the top before serving is delicious.

Coffee and Ginger Soufflé

The combination of coffee and ginger is excellent, providing a sophisticated dessert.

1 cup full-cream milk
3 tbsp coarsely ground medium-strength coffee
3 tbsp butter
4 tbsp flour
4 egg yolks
6 tbsp superfine sugar
3 tbsp chopped stem or crystallised ginger
5 egg whites and a pinch of salt
little confectioners sugar

Heat the milk with the coffee to boiling point, remove from the heat, cover and allow to infuse for several minutes, then strain. Melt the butter, stir in the flour and cook gently for a few minutes then gradually add the hot coffee-flavored milk, stirring constantly. Beat the egg yolks until pale then beat into the coffee base. Stir in sugar, then fold in chopped ginger. Whip egg whites with the pinch of salt to a stiff peak, fold one third into base to lighten, give whites another quick whisk, add to the base and fold in carefully. Turn soufflé into a scant 7 cups straight-sided ovenproof dish that has been well-buttered and sprinkled with sugar.

Bake in preheated oven at 400°F for about 30 minutes. The soufflé is done if it trembles rather than wobbles when gently shaken. Dust with confectioners sugar and serve immediately accompanied with light cream.

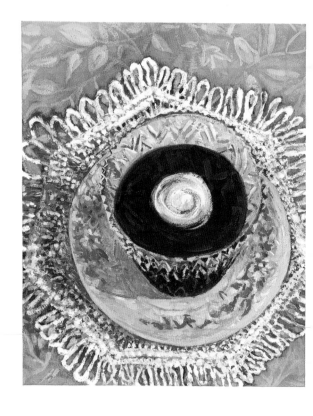

Coffee and Rum Jelly

Sparkling and light and very simple.

---

3 tbsp rum or coffee flavor liqueur
1 tbsp powdered gelatine
2 1/2 cups fresh, well-flavored coffee
sugar to taste
whipped cream to serve

Place the rum or liqueur in a cup or small dish, sprinkle the gelatine powder over and leave until granules have absorbed the liquid, about five minutes. Have the coffee freshly made and strained if necessary. Add the now transparent gelatine and stir into the coffee with sugar to taste until both are completely dissolved. Pour into clear glasses and chill until set. Serve with lightly whipped cream, either on the side or poured on top. Variations: The rum or liqueur can be omitted and the gelatine soaked in water. Also, the coffee can be infused with spices; use a piece of cinnamon bark, 2 cloves and 3 allspice berries, omit rum.

Coffee and Rum Mousse

A deliciously light mousse that marries the coffee and rum flavors marvellously.

---

4 tbsp light rum
1 tbsp powdered gelatine
1 cup freshly-made strong
medium roast coffee
3 egg yolks
6 tbsp superfine sugar
1 cup heavy cream
3 egg whites
(serves 6)

Sprinkle gelatine over rum and leave until the powder has absorbed the liquid, about five minutes. Strain the hot coffee, add the soaked gelatine and stir until completely dissolved. Beat the yolks until thick and pale, beat in the sugar until the mixture has increased in volume and is even paler. Gradually beat in the hot liquid and leave to cool. When the mixture has started to thicken, whip the cream until it almost holds its shape then fold in carefully. Whip the egg whites to soft peak and fold in as well. Pour mixture into a 5 cup mold, or individual dishes, and leave in a cold place to set. Alternatively, use a smaller, 3 cup mold with a paper collar tied firmly around its top. After the mousse has set, the collar can be removed, leaving the mixture standing proud of the dish, like a risen soufflé. Grated chocolate and/or whipped cream can be used to decorate the mousse. Instead of rum, cognac or kirsch can be used for flavoring.

Coffee Chiffon Tart

The crisp shell of this tart contrasts deliciously with a smooth and light filling, the coffee liqueur adding extra flavor.

Crust:	3 egg yolks
1⅓ cup chocolate Graham crackers, crushed	½ cup superfine sugar
	3 tbsp coffee essence
6 tbsp butter, melted	3 tbsp Tia Maria
Filling:	3 egg whites
1 tbsp powdered gelatine	**Garnish:**
4 tbsp water	grated chocolate
(serves 6–8)	

Stir together the crushed crackers and melted butter, then use to coat bottom and sides of a 9 x 1 inch deep tart pan or pie dish. Leave to set.

Sprinkle the gelatine over the water in a small saucepan and allow the powder to absorb the water, then heat very gently until the soaked gelatine has melted. Do not allow to boil.

Beat the egg yolks until thick and pale then gradually beat in the sugar until the mixture has swelled in volume and is even paler. Beat in coffee essence and Tia Maria spoon by spoon, then add the melted gelatine. As soon as mixture is on the point of setting, whip egg whites to a soft peak and fold in carefully. Fill the chocolate shell and leave in a cool place to set for at least 2 hours. Decorate with grated chocolate and serve with light cream if liked.

Bananas Tia Maria

A very easy dessert loved by everyone who likes bananas.

6 firm bananas
2 tbsp unsalted butter
4 tbsp soft brown sugar
4 tbsp Tia Maria

4 tbsp freshly made strong
black coffee
light cream to serve

Peel the bananas, cut in half lengthwise, place in an ovenproof dish. Melt the butter and pour over the bananas, rolling the fruit so each is covered in butter. Sprinkle the sugar over and place in a preheated oven at 325°F for 20 minutes, or until bananas are soft, then remove. Pour off all the juices into a small pan, keep the bananas hot, add the Tia Maria to the pan, set alight and douse with the coffee. Heat through and stir to amalgamate juices and coffee then pour back over the bananas. Serve immediately with light cream.

Chocolate Marquise
with Coffee Bean Sauce

This is a very rich but utterly delicious dessert that is transformed by the Coffee Bean Sauce.

3oz plain chocolate
4 large egg yolks
1/2 cup superfine sugar
3/4 cup unsalted butter, softened

36 lady fingers
5 tbsp strong black coffee
Sauce:
1 1/2 cups full-cream milk

²/₃ cup unsweetened cocoa powder, sifted

1¼ cups heavy cream

2 tbsp confectioners sugar, sifted

generous ½ cup superfine sugar

1½ tsp fresh, fine coffee grounds

5 medium size egg yolks

(serves 6–8)

Melt chocolate carefully in small bowl over simmering water then remove from heat. Beat egg yolks until pale and fluffy, add sugar gradually, continuing to beat until mixture very pale and thick. Beat in the melted chocolate. Cream butter until light and fluffy then gradually beat in the cocoa powder. Beat together with the chocolate mixture. In a large, chilled bowl, use a whisk to whip together the cream and the confectioners sugar until very light and thick, be careful not to overbeat. With the whisk, work cream mixture into the chocolate mixture until perfectly blended.

Line a 2 lb bread pan with waxed paper. Brush each lady finger with the coffee and use to line sides and bottom of pan or mold. Fill center with the chocolate mixture and chill in refrigerator for 2–3 hours.

For the sauce, place milk and half the sugar in a saucepan and bring to boiling point. Add the coffee grounds, cover, remove from heat and leave to infuse for 15 minutes. Beat egg yolks until pale and thick, add remaining sugar and beat again until increased in volume and even paler. Continue to beat while adding the milk and coffee mixture. Clean out saucepan, add custard mixture and cook over a very low heat, stirring constantly, until it thickens. To test: dip wooden spatula or spoon into mixture, hold up and run a finger across the custard. If channel remains clear, the custard is cooked. Do not let the custard boil or it will curdle. Cool, stirring.

Turn Marquise out onto serving plate and accompany with sauce.

Café Parfait

The best, the creamiest, the tastiest of ices.

---

1 cup light cream
4 tbsp medium ground coffee
4 egg yolks
1/2 cup superfine sugar
1 cup heavy cream

Heat light cream to boiling point, add the ground coffee, stir well, cover, remove from heat and leave to infuse for 15 minutes.

Beat the egg yolks until thick and pale, gradually beat in the sugar and continue beating until mixture forms a thick "ribbon" when the beater is held up. Continue to beat while adding the cream and coffee, then pour into a clean saucepan and cook gently over a very low heat, stirring all the time, until mixture is slightly thickened. To test: Dip wooden spoon or spatula into mixture, hold up and run a finger through the custard coating. If the channel remains clear, the custard is cooked. Strain custard into a bowl and leave to cool.

Beat heavy cream until it will nearly hold its shape then fold carefully into cooled custard mixture. Either freeze in ice cream maker or freeze in a metal tray, beating the mixture well once or twice as it freezes.

Granita al Caffe

The most refreshing of desserts, very popular in Italy. Make sure the coffee has a lively flavor.

> 4 cups freshly brewed strong coffee
> 8 tbsp superfine sugar
> 3 tbsp rum
> I cup whipping cream
> 2 tbsp confectioners sugar, sifted
> (serves 6)

Add the sugar to the hot coffee and stir until dissolved. Allow to cool then stir in the rum. Pour into large metal container, or containers, so that there is only a shallow depth of liquid as this will help speed the freezing. Place in freezer. When solid, plunge bottom of container into boiling water for a few seconds then turn out frozen coffee and break into pieces. Turn into small crystals in a food processor. Return to freezer until ready to serve. Whip cream with the confectioners sugar until it holds its shape. Remove crystals from freezer and, if necessary, briefly process again, then pile into six chilled serving glasses, top with whipped cream and serve immediately.

Walnut and Coffee Roulade

An impressive dessert that is always popular.

Roulade:	Filling:
5 large eggs, separated	3 egg yolks
generous ¹/₂ cup superfine sugar	scant ¹/₂ cup superfine sugar
scant cup walnuts, ground quite finely	3 tbsp cornstarch
	I cup boiling milk
2 tbsp cornstarch	I small pat of butter
	2 tbsp coffee essence
(serves 6)	

Line a Swiss roll pan approximately 13 x 8 inch with waxed paper. Beat egg yolks until pale then beat in sugar until thick and almost white. Mix ground walnuts with cornstarch and fold into beaten yolks. Whip egg white to stiff peak stage and fold into walnut mixture lightly but thoroughly. Pour into prepared pan and bake 20 minutes in oven preheated to 350°F until well risen, golden and resilient to touch. Turn out onto sheet of greaseproof paper sprinkled with sugar and remove lining paper (tear it off in strips if it starts to stick). Trim long edges with very sharp knife, roll roulade and paper up loosely together from one of the short ends and leave on rack to cool.

To make *crème pâtissière* filling, beat egg yolks then beat in sugar until the mixture is thick and pale. Beat in the cornstarch. Gradually pour on the boiling milk while continuing to beat. Pour mixture into clean saucepan and place over a medium heat. Bring to a boil while stirring continuously with a wire whisk but be careful mixture doesn't burn on bottom of the pan. After mixture has reached boiling point, lower heat and simmer very gently for 2–3 minutes, watching that it doesn't scorch. Then remove from heat and beat in a pat of butter with the coffee essence. Cover with plastic wrap and leave to cool.

When the filling is cold, carefully unroll the roulade, spread the *crème pâtissière* over and roll up again, making a firm pleat with the beginning then using the paper to pull the roll over, finally landing it on a serving dish (don't worry if the roll splits, it looks good with some of the filling oozing out). Sift a little confectioners sugar over before serving.·

Gâteau Malakoff au Café

Richest of all coffee puddings and quite irresistible.

praline made with 1 1/4 cups browned hazelnuts and 3/4 cup superfine sugar	3 tbsp best instant coffee dissolved in 5 tbsp water just off the boil
2 sticks unsalted butter, softened	2 cups whipping cream
1 1/3 cups confectioners sugar, sifted	27 lady fingers
1 large egg yolk	3 tbsp Tia Maria or Kahlua
	2/3 cup milk
	toasted almond halves

(serves 8–10)

Make praline by heating sugar over brisk heat until it first melts then turns brown. Add the nuts, stir well then turn out onto an oiled pan or piece of marble. Allow to cool completely then break into small bits and grind either in a food processor or small mill.

Cream butter then beat in sugar bit by bit until mixture is very light and fluffy. Beat in the egg yolk and then the coffee. Stir in the praline mixture. Whip the cream until it just holds its shape and fold carefully into the coffee butter icing.

Mix together the liqueur and the milk then briefly dip both sides of nine lady fingers and arrange them in threes on the base of an oblong serving dish; spread over a layer of the cream. Repeat with two more layers of biscuits and cream. Finally use the remaining cream to cover the sides of the block. Scatter the toasted almonds over the top then chill for several hours, preferably overnight, before serving.

Coffee Meringue Gâteau

A crisp and delectable gâteau to serve with coffee or tea or as a dessert.

Meringue:	2 tbsp medium ground coffee
1 cup superfine sugar	6 tbsp sugar
1 cup ground walnuts	4 large egg yolks
1 tbsp cornstarch	2 sticks
4 large egg whites	unsalted butter
Filling:	**Garnish:**
6 tbsp water	9 walnut halves
(serves 8)	

To make the meringue: Mix half the sugar with the ground walnuts and cornstarch (easiest in a food processor after grinding the nuts, but don't reduce to powder, they are nicest with plenty of texture). Whip the whites to stiff peak, then beat in the other half of the sugar by the tablespoonful. Finally, carefully fold in the mixture of sugar, nuts and cornstarch. Have three baking trays lined with waxed paper on which you have drawn three 8 inch rings. Divide the meringue mixture between these and carefully spread out to fill the circles. Bake in a preheated oven at 250°F for 1½ hours, until the meringues are slightly colored and will lift off the paper. Remove and cool on a wire rack, peeling off the paper.

To make the filling: Place the coffee grounds in a small saucepan with the water, bring just up to a boil, remove from the heat, cover and allow to infuse for five minutes. Strain the coffee, return to the cleaned out pan, add the sugar, heat gently until the sugar has melted then boil until the syrup will form a thread when tested between thumb and finger (236°F on a sugar thermometer). Beat the yolks until pale and thick then slowly add the hot syrup, beating all the time, then continue beating until the mixture has cooled.

Cream the butter then gradually add the egg mixture, beating all the time. Spread in between the meringue layers and all over the top and sides of the gâteau. Finish by sprinkling the gâteau with the toasted flaked almonds and chill for 2–3 hours before serving.

Coffee Mille Feuilles

12oz puff pastry	2 tbsp coffee, freshly ground
Filling:	1/3 cup heavy cream, chilled
3 egg yolks	3 tbsp confectioners sugar, sifted
4 tbsp sugar	**Icing:**
3 tbsp cornstarch	1 cup confectioners sugar, sifted
pinch salt	approx. 1 tbsp water
1 cup milk	1oz bitter chocolate

Roll out the puff pastry into a rectangle which, trimmed, will measure 8 x 18 inch and 1/10 inch thick. With a sharp, heavy knife cut into three identical strips, 6 x 8 inch. Place upside down on a large greased baking sheet brushed with water. Prick the strips all over with a fork to prevent them rising too much and bake in a preheated oven at 425°F for 20 minutes or until puffed and a good, hazelnut brown. Place pastry on a wire rack to cool.

To make the filling, beat egg yolks with sugar until thick and pale then beat in cornstarch and salt. Heat the milk with the coffee to boiling point, allow to infuse for 2 minutes then strain and pour into the beaten yolks and sugar, stirring constantly. Place in a clean saucepan and, stirring all the time over a medium heat, bring mixture to a boil. Lower heat and simmer carefully for 2–3 minutes until mixture thick and smooth, watch that it doesn't scorch on the bottom. Pour into a clean bowl and beat with a whisk until cool. Add the confectioners sugar to the chilled heavy cream and whisk in a chilled bowl until the mixture will almost hold its shape. Add the pastry cream and carefully fold both together.

To assemble: Place the strips of pastry on top of each other and trim the edges with a sharp knife. Then place on upside down on a rack and spread with half of the cream. Turn the second strip upside down and place on top, spread remaining cream on top and place last strip upside down on top, making sure it is quite level.

To ice: Melt chocolate. Stir sufficient water into the confectioners sugar to make a thick and smooth icing. Take out two tablespoons and add to the melted chocolate, stir together well then place in small paper bag and cut a tiny piece off the corner to make a piping hole. Spread the white icing over the top puff pastry layer then squeeze lines of chocolate icing across the top, $^1/_2$ inch apart. Run a wet skewer across the lines in alternate directions, 1 inch apart. Leave to set, then serve.

Coffee and Walnut Cake

Many years ago, Fullers in England sold a coffee and walnut cake with a white frosted icing. The following recipe brings back memories of that very popular cake.

generous $^1/_2$ cup butter, softened	2 egg whites
1 cup superfine sugar	**Frosting:**
2 egg yolks	1$^1/_2$ cups sugar
3 tbsp coffee essence	4 tbsp water
$^3/_4$ cup walnuts, roughly chopped	$^1/_4$ tsp cream of tartar
$^1/_2$ cup milk	pinch salt
2 cups flour sifted with 3 tsp	2 egg whites
baking powder and a	**Garnish:**
pinch salt	8 walnut halves

Cream the butter then beat in the sugar until mixture very light and fluffy. Beat in egg yolks and coffee essence then the chopped walnuts. Fold in the flour and milk, together, in three lots. Whip whites to soft peak and fold carefully into the mixture. Pour into two round greased 8inch sandwich pans and bake in preheated oven at 375°F for 20–30 minutes, until risen and springy. Leave in pan for five minutes then turn out onto wire rack to cool.

To make the frosting: Mix together the sugar, water, cream of tartar, salt and egg white, stirring until sugar dissolved, then place over a pan of simmering water and beat until the mixture will stand in peaks. Remove bowl from heat and continue beating as the mixture cools until it is stiff enough to spread. Spread a little less than half the mixture on one of the cake halves, top with the other half then spread remaining frosting all over cake. Decorate with the walnut halves and leave to set.

Coffee Macaroons

These unusual macaroons are as delectably moist as toothsome.

²/₃ cup ground almonds	1¹/₂ tbsp arrowroot or rice flour
1¹/₂ cups superfine sugar	¹/₂ tsp vanilla essence
4 tbsp instant coffee powder	rice paper
(grind coffee granules)	split almonds
3 egg whites, lightly beaten	
to break up	
(makes 16)	

Mix together the almonds, sugar and coffee powder. Add the egg whites and beat together well. Stir in the arrowroot or rice flour and the vanilla essence. Place rice paper on baking sheets then spoon on level tablespoons of mixture, spreading out to about 2 inch across. Leave plenty of room between the rounds for further spreading. Add a split almond in the middle of each round. Bake in a preheated oven at 350°F for about 20 minutes. Leave to cool on the baking sheet then break off rice paper around each macaroon and store them in an airtight tin.

Coffee Banana Bread

Somewhere between a loaf and a cake, this is a useful and tasty teatime treat that can be served with or without butter.

---

2 cups self-rising flour, sifted with pinch of salt	4 tbsp very strong black coffee
½ cup butter, diced	2 ripe bananas, mashed
1¼ cups soft brown sugar	2 large eggs, lightly beaten
2 tbsp roughly chopped walnuts	2 tsp ground coffee mixed with 2 tbsp demerara sugar

---

Rub the butter into the flour with fingertips until the mixture resembles breadcrumbs, stir in the sugar and the chopped walnuts. In another bowl, mix together the coffee, mashed bananas and eggs then mix this with dry ingredients, stirring until you have a smooth mixture. Line a greased 2 lb (9 x 5 inch) loaf pan with a strip of non-stick baking paper, covering the bottom and ends, and pour in the mixture. Sprinkle the mixture of ground coffee and demerara sugar on top and bake in a preheated oven at 350°F for 1 – 1¼ hours or until the cake is springy to the touch and an inserted skewer emerges clean. Allow to cool in the pan then store in an airtight container. The loaf is best the day after baking.

Coffee and Rum Truffles

The finishing touch to a great meal.

7oz bitter chocolate
2 tbsp rum
4 tsp coffee essence
3½ fl oz heavy cream
2–3 tbsp confectioners sugar, sifted
cocoa powder
(makes approx. 24)

Melt chocolate with rum and coffee essence in a bowl over a pan of simmering water. Remove from heat, gradually beat in cream and then confectioners sugar to taste. Allow to cool, then beat until mixture has the consistency of thick cream, and will stand in peaks. Refrigerate until stiff enough to shape into balls. Toss teaspoons of mixture in cocoa powder and between palms of hands roll in more cocoa. Keep in fridge and consume within one week.

Index